Lau—
Happy
Birthday!
Love,
miss Kitty

A GLIMPSE INTO THE LIVES

OF NEW YORK'S

FELINE INHABITANTS

FELINES OF

NEW YORK

JIM TEWS

Simon & Schuster Paperbacks

New York   London   Toronto   Sydney   New Delhi

Simon & Schuster Paperbacks
An Imprint of Simon & Schuster, Inc.
1230 Avenue of the Americas
New York, NY 10020

First Simon & Schuster trade paperback edition November 2015

SIMON & SCHUSTER PAPERBACKS and colophon are registered trademarks of Simon & Schuster, Inc.

For information about special discounts for bulk purchases, please contact Simon & Schuster Special Sales at 1-866-506-1949 or business@simonandschuster.com.

The Simon & Schuster Speakers Bureau can bring authors to your live event. For more information or to book an event, contact the Simon & Schuster Speakers Bureau at 1-866-248-3049 or visit our website at www.simonspeakers.com.

Interior design by Joy O'Meara

Manufactured in the United States of America

1 3 5 7 9 10 8 6 4 2

Library of Congress Cataloging-in-Publication data is available.

ISBN 978-1-5011-2583-6
ISBN 978-1-5011-2584-3 (ebook)

This book is dedicated to all the cats in the world.

I do your bidding now.

INTRODUCTION

Some time ago I was walking by a clowder of feral cats in Williamsburg when one of them said to me, "Hey, you should take my picture and ask me a few questions. Then post the picture and excerpts from that interview on a website. Maybe you could turn that into a book."

"I think someone's already doing that with humans," I said.

"Yeah, but it would be way funnier with cats."

I had my camera and I'd never heard a cat speak, let alone make a specific request, so I obliged. After photographing and interviewing hundreds of cats over several months, I realized that each one of them has a story to tell. Most of those stories involve birds and make little sense, but many of them give a view of New York I'd never been privy to. I hope these cats and their stories will give you the same. And if they don't, then just enjoy the pictures, I guess.

My grandparents immigrated here from New Jersey with nothing, and now I have this box. I wish they could see me. They'd be, like, "How the fuck did you get that box? We never had a box." But I don't know, the box just kind of showed up, so I sat in it.

—JEDDY, Lower East Side

I believe climate change is real, but I don't like to think about it. I mean, what if the ocean slowly swallows Manhattan? If the environmental damage caused by humans results in me getting wet, I'm not going to be okay with that.

—MILO, Upper East Side

My biggest regret is not finishing college or getting any sort of formal degree. Just imagine where I'd be with a decent grad school education. I wouldn't be sitting on this chair, that's for sure. I'd probably be sitting in a much nicer chair.

—DIDID, Greenpoint

I work from home, which can make me a little stir-crazy. It's important to socialize with anything you can find. Like, sometimes I'll talk to the couch or to the northeast corner of the apartment. If you don't make time for stuff like that, you'll go nuts.

—EMMA, Williamsburg

A lot of people think we hate Mondays, but that's a dangerous stereotype reinforced by the media. We actually have no idea what day it is.

—CHARLIE, Bed-Stuy

Can you really trust anyone? I mean, how do you know?
I guess if they're offering you food, then they're probably
okay, but that's really the only way you can tell.

So, if someone gives you food, you automatically trust him?

If it's wet food or real tuna, then yeah, of course. Dry food?
Not so much.

—WESLEY, Bushwick

13

They've been working on this building across from us for quite a while. The whole block is under construction constantly. I would worry that we're going to get priced out of this neighborhood, but I don't pay rent, the guy does. So it's kind of his problem.

—TOBY, Midtown

We were in Italy once.
I remember it pretty vividly.
I sat on a really old sofa most
of the time.

*You don't remember anything
else about living in Italy?*

I wasn't allowed outside.

—NANCY, Williamsburg

You don't want to get too hung up on your own image, your ego. You just have to do what works for you and realize that others are usually in their own heads, worried about themselves. So they're not really going to care if you're doing something weird. Because they're probably doing something weird, too.

—TRIPP, Midtown

19

I've never been in a real fight, which makes me feel like I've never been tested. I'm also kind of a pacifist, so I try to avoid violence. But sometimes I wonder how I'd do if I got in a jam.

What do you think you'd do?

Well, I can jump crazy high. So if, like, I was being chased by some older cats, I wouldn't have to fight them. I'd just jump onto something they couldn't jump onto. Then I'd be, like, "Hey, why are we fighting? We're all cats here. There're enough toys for everybody."

—OSCAR, Bushwick

I know every corner of this apartment really well, so if something's moving around in here that shouldn't be moving around in here, I'll find it. Then I'll decide its fate, but I am a fair and just cat. I understand my power.

—OYSTER, Williamsburg

Sometimes I sit really still so people think I'm a decoration. Watch, I'll do it now. Then tell me if you thought I was a decoration.

That's impressive, but I don't think it will work on me, because I know you're not a decoration.

But you will, just watch . . . See, you thought I was a decoration. Didn't you?

Um . . . sure.

Told you.

—NORA, Greenpoint

We took a car ride this one time. Me, the woman, the man, and the other cat I live with, Bill. I thought we were going to the vet, but we ended up just going to this other house for a few days. I don't think I've ever been more relieved in my life. Every time we get in the car, I hope we're going to that other house, but we always end up going to the vet.

—PETE, Upper West Side

Did Pete tell you that story about going to the vet every time we get in the car? He doesn't know what he's talking about. We go to the other house twice a year for vacation, and we go to the vet about as frequently. He's just being dramatic. Good guy, but a little dramatic.

—BILL, Upper West Side

Family is everything to me, but our family isn't traditional. It's made up of two people, a dog, and another cat. We've all been together since I can remember.

Is the other cat your sibling?

No, actually, funny story. We thought we were siblings, but then this one day we were bored, so I said to him, "Hey, Jefferson, do you think we look alike?"

He said, "I don't know. Tell me what I look like."

I said, "You're gray with some white and your hair is kind of short."

And he said, "You don't look like that at all. Your hair is long and you're, like, orange and white."

We were both kind of, like, "What the . . . ?" But we didn't think much more of it because we're family, and family doesn't always mean you're from the same litter.

—MR. PEEPERS, Bushwick

29

At a certain point in life you just kind of get bored with the things that used to fire you up. It's not a bad thing, it just means you're maturing and your priorities are changing. You gain perspective. You start thinking, "Do I really need to chase this thing? Or should I just chill here and think about things? I'll chill here and think about things." That's growth.

—JEFFERSON, Bushwick

31

I heard this mouse on the floor and I was, like, "Not in my house!" Then I killed it. Pretty quick, too.

That mouse there? That's a toy.

No, it's not, it's a dead mouse. It's been dead for months.

Okay.

—TANOOKI, Astoria

People don't sleep enough, and they all seem to be hunting something that can't be caught. You think you're the dominant species just because you go to the bathroom in a bowl instead of a box. But who's cleaning up after whom?

—SOSUEME, Williamsburg

A man in this building feeds us. He also built a little shelter outside. He doesn't realize that's where we've been plotting our takeover.

Your takeover?

I've said too much.

—NAME WITHHELD, Staten Island

I'm learning how to cook!

Who's teaching you how to cook?

We watch the shows all the time. You don't think I've absorbed
some of that knowledge? On Sunday I'm broiling some cod.
I've been planning it for a while. Just have to get the cod,
reach the oven knobs, put the cod on the pan, open the oven,
close the oven, count for a while, then open the oven,
get it out of the oven, wait for it to cool, then eat it.

Sounds like you've got it all figured out.

I've seen the woman do it and it looks pretty simple.
But she has a much easier time grabbing things than I do.
So I'm not going to say this won't be a challenge.
Also, I'm not sure where to get cod.

—GOGO, Greenpoint

I met the president when I was younger, or maybe it was just a guy that called himself the president. I have no real way of verifying that sort of thing.

—BRINDLE, Williamsburg

Sometimes I come in here to think.

—PEARL, Astoria

When I don't fit in here, then I know it's time to get a little more active. They always think I'm hiding, but I'm actually just making sure I stay healthy.

—GOLDBERG, Long Island City

44

The lady brought these empty boxes home and I thought, "Finally, some real furniture." But then she said we were moving to California. She seems kind of stressed about it. I just want the boxes to be empty again.

—CLEO, Williamsburg

47

I've learned so many things in my life, but learning how to make people do everything for me was probably the most valuable.

—MANFACE, Ridgewood

We moved here because New York had an amazing live music scene. It's a lot of electronic kid shit now. But whatever, loud noises terrify me anyway.

—NALA, Williamsburg

51

A lot of people are scared of me. It's the whole Halloween/witch/bad luck thing. Will I bring you bad luck if I walk past you? No, of course not. But if you think that, then you'll probably manifest it.

So you believe in positive thinking?

Yeah, I'm a big believer in positive thinking. Like, I start to think, "I'm getting hungry. There should be food in that bowl." Then fifteen minutes later, the woman puts food in the bowl. It happened because I believed it would happen.

—TOE, Chinatown

53

After my first divorce, I kind of decided to protect myself a little more. I've been sticking to it so far. I'll get out there again eventually.

You've been divorced? No offense, but I didn't even know cats could marry.

Don't be ignorant.

—MAEBE, Cobble Hill

I decided a long time ago that I don't want kittens.
A lot of other cats judge me for it, but kittens
would just get in the way of my career.

What career is that?

I'm in the business of walking around and lying on stuff.
It's insanely competitive.

—ORANGE, Park Slope

When we're done with this, I want you to brush me.

You're not my cat.

What does that have to do with anything?

—MISS KITTY, SoHo

Nope.

—BEAKER, Williamsburg

I thought for a while that I wanted to be a musician, but then I started producing. Touching the knobs and sliders and all that. It's my calling. I don't get credited, but that's not why I do it. I do it because I love walking across electronic equipment.

—LORETTA, Crown Heights

I'm a descendant of lions, so sometimes I'll get real wild-animal urges. Like, I want to just hunt something.

What do you hunt?

String, mostly.

—SCOUT, Greenpoint

I have a crush on this stray that lives down the block from us, but the other cats she hangs out with give me a hard time. And they look super tough. I've been trying to leave the door open so maybe she walks in and the guy I live with ends up keeping her. But then what if she doesn't like me? I haven't really thought this through.

—GARY, Ridgewood

I've kind of claimed this table as my own. I'll let the woman and her friends eat here, but only if she feeds me first. And I won't let the other cat up here. I've heard the woman call me territorial. I have no idea what that means. I just know that I'm adamant about keeping others out of spaces I've claimed as my own.

—LENNY, Williamsburg

We've been together for five years. But we haven't spoken in weeks.

Why aren't you speaking?

I shit outside the litter box and let him take the blame.

—SARTRE and SIMONE, *Little Italy*

If I could have one wish, it would be to change the channel.

—GEORGE, Williamsburg

I've been thinking about going back to school. In criminal justice. What I'm doing now just seems to be getting me nowhere.

What are you doing now?

What does it look like I'm doing?

—TAIKO, Bushwick

I actually have to use the can right now, but we can talk afterward if you still want to.

—SAL, Ridgewood

I can see some really expensive condos from here. I'd like to get in one and scratch the shit out of some really nice furniture, maybe piss on something. I don't know, I like to dream big.

—CARL, Williamsburg

You saw that mouse, right?

—CAM, Williamsburg

80

I used to be an indoor cat, but the kid left the door open and I got out. I was just waiting for the right moment. That kid was kind of a jerk, a real whisker-puller.

—SAM, Williamsburg

I was the CEO of a Fortune 500 company.

What happened?

They found out I was a cat.

—VANCE, Williamsburg

85

This boot is my father. He's not very expressive. He has a hard time being open, but I love him anyway.

—ARTHUR, Ridgewood

I don't like keeping secrets. I'm a big proponent of just letting it all hang out. Letting people know who you are and what you've done. Like, I'll tell you right now, even though we just met, I stole the cap from the milk jug this morning when the girl left it on the counter. I hid it under the bed. I could've just gone without saying that; nobody would've known it was me. I feel better about it now, though.

Do you want me to tell the girl for you?

Please.

—AURON, Lower East Side

I've never modeled before, so this is kind of a new thing for me.

You can relax; you're not modeling. I'm just photographing you as you naturally are.

But I could be a model, right? You think I should model?

Um, yeah, I guess—if you want to.

—CHLOE, Williamsburg

When I had a kitten, everything changed.
I can't just pick up and go like I used to.

Where would you go?

I don't know. Wherever. The other rooms, mostly.

—MICHELLE, the Bronx

I want to make sure she knows everything she needs to survive in here. Like how to catch the feather thing. And how to look warm and indifferent at the same time.

—MICHELLE and JOONEY, the Bronx

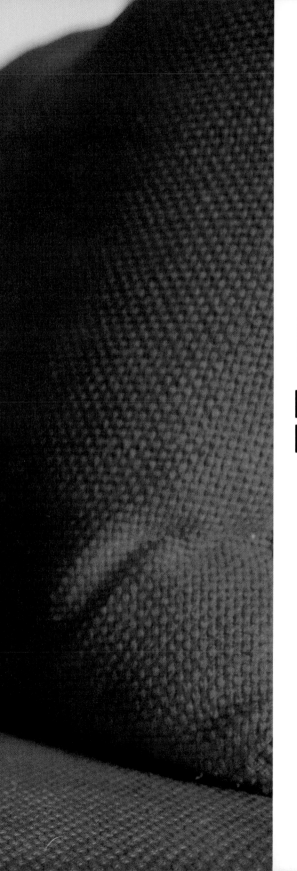

I don't like being picked up, but it keeps happening.

—JOONEY, the Bronx

I used to squat in this house on 110th Street. Me and a bunch of other cats, when we were younger. But then I just hit that point where I decided it wasn't the life I wanted, so I let someone catch me.

—JONES, Harlem

The idea of going on a crazy road trip sounds like so much fun, but the reality of it is terrifying. I'm not sure why dogs seem so into it.

—BAMFORD, Long Island City

Sometimes I wish I could use a smartphone. I wouldn't use it for games or social media or anything, though. That seems like a waste of time.

What would you use it for?

I'd use it to order food.

—HONEYDEW, Lower East Side

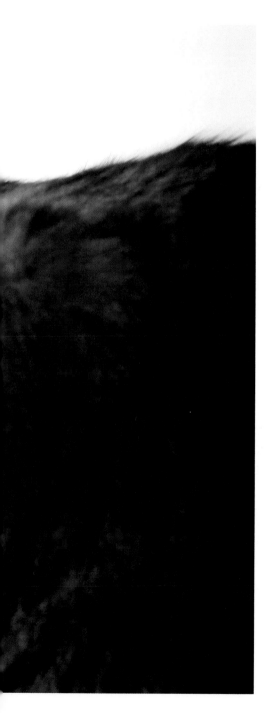

When I was younger, a friend and I chased down this bird. We didn't hurt it, but we scared it pretty bad. My friend was, like, "Kill it!" but I just couldn't. That's when I realized I was a little more sensitive than most cats. I've killed bugs, though. I'll ruin a bug's day without a second thought. Fuck bugs.

—SKIP, Staten Island

Sometimes I think these toys are being controlled by the guy. But other times I'm, like, "No, that's definitely moving on its own." It's just one of those things I don't think I'll ever figure out.

—BOBBI, Harlem

I don't know how I lost this arm, honestly. I didn't even realize it was missing until I saw the other cat that lives here. I was, like, "Hey, how did you get that extra one?" And he was, like, "Extra one?" Then we kind of figured it out together. I felt bad about it for a minute, but I can still jump pretty high. So whatever.

—ALMA, Astoria

Self-improvement is a constant for me. Every time I wake up, which is several times a day, I say, "Maddie, how can we improve Maddie today, right now, this minute?" Then I'll do something like stretch or drink some water.

That's how you better yourself?

Yes, if you are stiff and dehydrated, you are not being your best self. Nap, stretch, hydrate. Stay present.

—MADDIE, Financial District

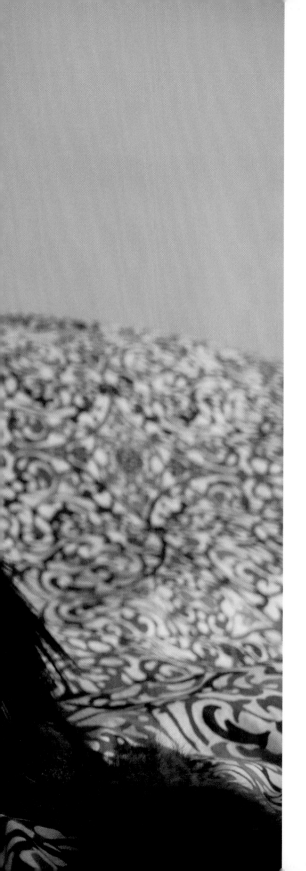

Whenever there are strangers in the house, I try not to talk to them. Unless they stay for more than an hour or two. Then I'll probably come out, make sure everything's cool. But I'm not going to let you pet me until I see you a second or third time. It's a personal policy.

—BANJO, Bed-Stuy

113

You know, I do my best to make recommendations, but often my suggestions are perceived as aggression. I have good intentions. I just don't want you people reading garbage, that's all.

—TINY THE USURPER, Park Slope

115

I'm not entirely familiar with the Internet thing. Like, I've heard of it, but I've never watched it or smelled it or whatever you do to the Internet. I've heard it's full of cats, though. Is that true?

Yeah, pretty much. It's, like, ninety percent cat stuff.

Whoa.

—SHAMU, Brooklyn Heights

We're doing you all a favor here. Do you have any idea what kinds of rodent problems this park would have if we weren't here to chase those little monsters down? And we're here if you want to come look at us, you know? You want to teach your kids about animals, but don't want to pay for the zoo? Bring 'em here. We're good guys, is what I'm saying.

—JARVIS, Morningside Heights

I've been taking classes at Columbia.

—BENNY, Morningside Heights

Everything the light touches is our kingdom.

Ha-ha, yeah. Like from **The Lion King** *movie.*

Never seen it.

—ENID, Morningside Heights

When I was doing my artist-in-residency program in Cassis, that's when I was at my happiest. I was young, unattached, unburdened. Just living for my work.

Why can't you do that now?

I'm just too comfortable here.

—MARGOT, Park Slope

I know I have it better than a lot of cats because of the girl
that lives here, and I want to show how grateful I am.
I just have such a huge problem saying thank you.

Why's that?

Because every noise I make kind of sounds the same.

—MISKO, Upper East Side

When you're a cat, like me, there's this constant balancing act you're doing when you interact with people. You're always asking yourself, "How much of a person's behavior do I have to tolerate in order to get access to their food?"

—KIP, Gramercy

I went to the vet last week for the third time I can remember.

Was everything okay?

I was given a clean bill of health, but I was not okay. Have you ever been to the vet? It's never okay.

What would make going to the vet less of a horrible experience?

If they could just do everything they need to do without touching me, that would help.

—FINN, Park Slope

If I feel like eating flowers, I'll eat flowers. Everyone gets weird about it, but whatever. When an urge to do something hits, if you're not hurting anyone, then just do it. Eat some fucking flowers if you wanna eat flowers.

—NORMAN, Bushwick

I was in love once, but we weren't together very long. He was a Himalayan the woman brought in for a few weeks as a favor to her friend. It was quite a whirlwind affair. We just lay in the sun and did a lot of catnip together. He wore a bell on his collar. If I ever heard that bell again, I don't know what I'd do. I'd probably make a noise to get his attention, but then I'd keep walking away from him every time he came toward me. I've never been one to show vulnerability. My god, I can't believe I'm telling you this. It sounds so ridiculous.

—PETIE, Gramercy

135

I like to make sure every customer leaves here satisfied. I make sure they find what they're looking for, and that they pet me. If they don't find what they're after, that's okay. As long as they pet me.

—MISTY, Park Slope

137

You'd think living in a place like this would be a dream, and sometimes it is. But more often it's like working at an amusement park where you've ridden all the rides.

—MINA, Park Slope

I'm trying to get a business plan together for my start-up. I'm a little worried about how I'm going to fund it, though. It's been tough to find investors. I walked into a bank last week in the hopes of getting a loan, but no luck.

What's your start-up?

I'm developing a multiplatform app that helps you find single cats in your area that are looking to hook up. It's called Littr.

—HAMMIE, Upper East Side

I never really liked traveling.
Staying in one place is
underrated.

—MARS, Chelsea

I once gave a lecture on urban policy and planning and its effects on the feline population of Manhattan. No one listened.

—MINTA, Upper West Side

I've never been to a restaurant before. It's one of those things I've always wanted to do.

People feed you regularly. That's kind of like going to a restaurant.

But it's not the full experience. There's no atmosphere, no presentation, no wine pairings. I've seen it on TV. I want the whole thing.

—JUNO, Park Slope

I haven't received a birthday present in a few years now. Which is fine, because I stopped counting my birthdays a while ago. I'm not really concerned with the passing of time in general.

—DIEGO, Fort Greene

149

I've got plenty of toys, sure. But I'd trade them all in, in a second, for one real bug.

—SASHA, Upper West Side

For me, showing love is more about what I won't do than what I will do. For example, if I love you, I won't shit outside your bedroom door.

—LOLO, Park Slope

I used to be a big hider. Couches, boxes, corners, closets, buckets, wherever. I'd hide anywhere. Then I hit this point in my life where I was, like, "Margaux, why are you hiding? These people only want to feed you and pet you. That's all they want. Come out and accept it." I did, and now here I am. Pet me.

—MARGAUX, Lower East Side

I can play all of these instruments.

Really?

Yeah, but it doesn't sound as good as when the girl plays them.
I have terrible rhythm.

—HAZEL, Union Square

Thankfully, I'm from the new generation. We know it's good to talk things out and to actually show emotions. I go to counseling once a week. I journal, too. My next step is watercolors. Painting just seems so soothing.

—MR. BOJANGLES, Astoria

If you're thinking about moving to New York, don't. The city's full.

—MISS PRISSY, Chelsea

The girl says we live in New York because there's always something to do.

Do you agree?

Yeah. I've never been bored here. I can always find a bottle cap or a piece of dirt to play with. I don't think you get that anywhere else.

—CASTIEL, East Village

We were worshiped in ancient Egypt. Now what are we? What do we have? I can't even open this screen door. Look away.

—ELISE, Astoria

Every time the woman orders Thai food, I say to her,
"Please get me a small pad thai," but she never does.
I had it once and I've been thinking about it ever since.

—FERRIS, Williamsburg

I'm not crazy about this haircut, but I'm owning it. That's the great thing about New York. Everyone's more worried about themselves than they are about you. I could literally walk around with a box on my head, and if I did it with enough swagger, people would ask me where I got the box so they could start doing the same.

—BUSTER, SoHo

169

If I wasn't here, this place would shut down completely. I mean, maybe it wouldn't shut down, but these papers would probably blow away. I know that much.

—COPY, Park Slope

This is my safe space. I've tried to get some boxes and my food under here, but the woman isn't really into it.

(Laughs) Is this where you have your mail delivered?

That's my ultimate goal.

—JASPER, Williamsburg

You never know where you'll end up in this life. You just have to make sure you're able to look yourself in the eye when you get there. Find a mirror and look yourself in the eye. Say, "We did it. We stayed on the straight and narrow, and now we're here." Now I'm here, looking in this mirror at what I once thought was another cat, but was actually me the whole time.

—STEVE, Lower East Side

175

I'm working on getting my real estate license. The housing market here is incredible, and it doesn't seem like it's going to end any time soon.

—LIAM, Williamsburg

I invented the telephone.

You did not invent the telephone.

—WHITNEY, Ridgewood

179

I've been out here pounding the pavement to raise awareness for some cat causes that are so often overlooked.

Cat causes?

See, exactly. This is exactly why I do what I do.

—NICK, Bushwick

You can't take just any cat and say, "Here, go live in New York." It's a special place for special cats. You have to have the wherewithal to live in a small space for a lot of money. And you have to learn how to watch a lot of people walk past your window. They'll tap on the glass sometimes, too. And you just have to be, like, *whatever* about it. It's a tough place.

—BIRD, Fort Greene

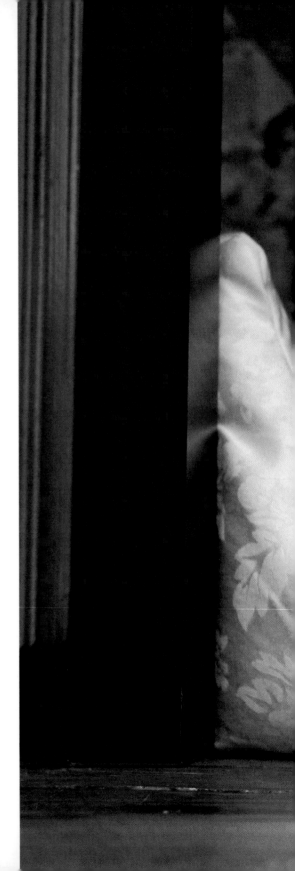

You hit this point in your life, as you get older, where the things you used to want are right in front of you. But you've just emotionally moved past them.

—BOBBY, Ridgewood

184

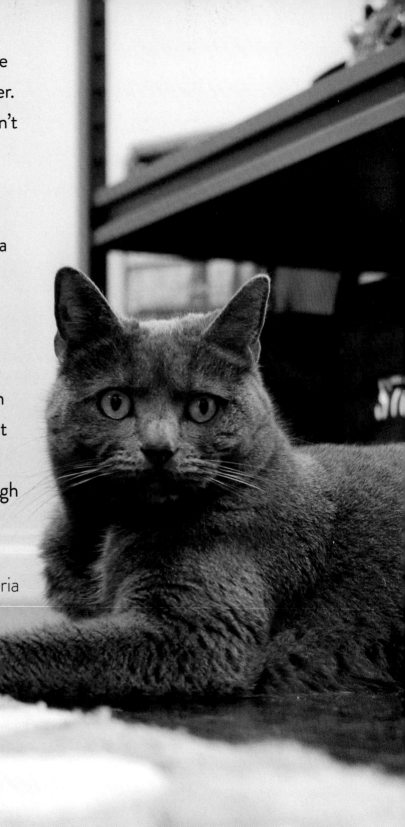

I spent a lot of time on the streets when I was younger. Just going places I shouldn't be. Chasing whatever moved. All that typical young-neighborhood-cat stuff. I got mixed up with a gang for a while.

You were in a gang?

Yeah, I don't talk to them anymore, though. I'm just not about that life. Too much violence, not enough furniture.

—DOT, Astoria

If you can't get the shot from back there, then you're not getting the shot.

Can I ask you some questions?

Well, that was already one question, so I'll give you one more. Go.

What's your biggest regret?

Not hiding better when I saw you walk in here.

—DOUG, Clinton Hill

189

I've never been in a relationship
that's lasted longer than a few meals.

—NERO, Sunnyside

You should touch this blanket; it's incredibly soft.
Don't touch me, though. Just the blanket.

—NOODLE, Williamsburg

I found an incredibly rare coin in the couch cushions once. I grabbed it, but then it slipped. And I think it's still in there, but I'm not sure. I think about that coin a lot. I could've sold that coin, maybe pawned it. I would've used the money to buy a sailboat. I really want a sailboat. Does that sound ridiculous?

Oh, no, not at all. There's nothing ridiculous about a cat wanting a sailboat.

Thank you. Finally someone gets me.

—NONI, Astoria

I wish I was a car.

You mean you wish you had a car?

No, I said, I wish . . . I *was* . . . a car.

—FUDGIE, Park Slope

I like being a little mysterious. I don't mind admitting that. If you show your cards right away, then what reason does anyone have to stick around and figure you out? Throw a wild paw every so often, keep 'em guessing.

—PHYLLIS, Williamsburg

You ever heard of the Canary Islands?

Yes, I hear it's beautiful.

I'm going there when I get out. Just a sunny island with a shit ton of birds. What a goddamn dream.

—SHEBA, Lower East Side

You don't get a powerful title and a corner office by just showing up and expecting it. You have to work for it. Be competitive. Be a little better than the rest. Read a lot, eat healthy, get some business cards that say, "I'm the boss," or something like that. That's how you become the boss.

—OLIVIA, Upper East Side

We live and work together, which would be tough on anyone, including the most even-keeled. But we make it work because we respect each other's space.

—CHARLES, Chelsea

I stare far into the distance and I dream. I dream about a world without Charles. I get happy thinking about the freedom, but sad thinking about the loneliness. I just wish he wasn't such a noisy eater.

—BIGGIE, Chelsea

You can't judge people by what neighborhood they live in, but everyone tries to. When people find out where I'm from, they're, like, "Why don't you have a beard and some cool glasses? Where's your record collection?" I'm, like, "Can't grow a beard, don't need glasses, record collection's on a shelf in the living room." Now let's talk about what really defines someone: poultry blend or seafood blend?

—MR. PRESIDENT, Greenpoint

I kicked three dudes out of a party we had here last week. I circled their legs until they got the point. I just wasn't into the vibe they were putting out. I like maintaining a good energy.

—ELIZA, Long Island City

I'm going to be a famous artist.

What kind of art do you make?

Found-object sculpture, mostly. I do stuff with socks, feathers, and dust bunnies.

—BEA, West Village

I've rubbed up against pretty much everything in this entire apartment. So it's all mine now, technically.

—GWYNETH, Bushwick

When I was about six months old, I found a cherry that rolled under the couch. I played with it for, like, three days. Then the man threw it out because it got kind of gross. But those were the best three days of my life.

—OMAR, Flatbush

I'm not much of a reader, but I feel like I've absorbed a lot of the stuff that comes through here. You know, you sit on the book for a while, you're going to soak up what's inside. It's just science.

—HAMPTON, Upper East Side

I fucking hate parties.

—MIMI, Williamsburg

I don't want to sound like I'm materialistic, but New York City is *the* place to live if you like shopping bags.

—REGINALD, Midtown

I just want to be taken seriously.

—LONDON, Astoria

There is definitely a fly on that wall behind you, and I definitely do not want to lose sight of it. So just bear with me for a minute. I'm more than happy to talk to you; I just have to keep an eye on it. I'm not being rude; it's not up to me, it's instinctual. Very sorry.

—TIGG, Park Slope

Wherever I end up, I'll be fine. I don't mean to sound cold, but I can adapt to pretty much anything. It's why we're going to outlast you as a species. You're looking at me like I just blew your mind.

—JUICE, Upper East Side

I'm kind of over being a cat.

Seriously? You have an incredible life.

It's nice, it's relaxing, but there's not
a lot of upward mobility.

—CHARLIE, Brooklyn Heights

This shoelace is my only earthly possession. I'm somewhat of a minimalist, which is necessary when you live in a place like New York City. It's the kind of city you come to with only one shoelace to your name, and you work hard. You work your ass off. In a few years, you have two or three shoelaces to your name. Then you move to the suburbs because you don't have enough room for more than three shoelaces.

—PHOEBE, Williamsburg

ACKNOWLEDGMENTS

Thanks to Chenoa Estrada for all her help and support, to Rick Ritter for letting me borrow better lenses, and to my family and friends who helped the website along. And of course a huge thanks to all the people who let a strange man from the Internet into their places to take pictures of their cats.

ABOUT THE AUTHOR

JIM TEWS is a comedian, writer, and now, somehow, a cat photographer. He lives in Queens with his girlfriend, Chenoa, and their two cats, Bea and Arthur. Everyone gets along pretty well.